The ParKit Golf Book of

Fun Golf Games for Kids

Maximize Learning Potential Through Fun and Exciting Golf Games

Imagination in a kit™

www.parkitgolf.com

Published by ARD Publishing
Boca Raton, Florida

Printed in the United States of America

Text and cover design by Rick Heard

"Imagination in a kit" is a trademark of ParKit Golf, Inc.

ISBN: 0-9786717-8-3
ISBN-13: 978-0-9786717-8-5

OVERVIEW

The ParKit Golf Book of Fun Golf Games for Kids is a compilation of 25 individual and team golf games that kids love to play. Through the fun and excitement of playing these fantastic games, kids of all ages learn the techniques and fundamentals of all of the major elements of golf. Far beyond simply competing with others and themselves, kids will learn to control their golf ball in putting, chipping, pitching, bunkers, and full swing shots. And, in playing the games, they will learn golf etiquette, sportsmanship and respect for others.

The games include both individual and team competitions that convert ordinary, boring practice exercises into fun activities that help kids learn golf fundamentals without realizing they are being taught.

Each game is explained in clear language that is simple to follow and understand. The games are appropriate for junior golf camps, group programs, and even for individual students with supervision by a parent or golf professional. Many of the games may be played in an open field or other location if a golf course practice facility is not available.

The ParKit Golf Book of Fun Golf Games for Kids reflects the experience and wisdom of the ParKit Golf team. Owned and operated by PGA golf professionals and staff with a passion for junior golf, ParKit Golf is the authoritative source for products, services and information related to junior golf instruction. With more than 90 years of combined experience in creating and teaching innovative junior golf programs to thousands of junior golfers, ParKit Golf represents one of the most experienced junior golf leadership teams in the world.

www.parkitgolf.com

TABLE OF CONTENTS

www.parkitgolf.com

INTRODUCTION

In our years of teaching junior golfers in camps, group classes, birthday parties, individual lessons and more, we have also learned many lessons ourselves. The most important of these lessons fall into two broad categories: safety and success.

Safety comes first, and wherever possible, we have designed the games in *The ParKit Golf Book of Fun Golf Games for Kids* with safety in mind. For example, each game includes a place for players to wait until it is their turn to hit. Frequently, this place is a cone that marks the "on deck" area. This simple but important part of each game provides the instructor with a specific place for players who are not swinging. While awaiting their turn, players should stand in that place quietly and orderly, respecting the player or players who are hitting. And, they should hold their clubs by the club head to minimize the chance of injury to another player.

We strongly encourage instructors to use these features of the games to bring order and control to the game situation. We have a "zero tolerance" attitude when it comes to safety and general good golf etiquette, yet our kids have a blast playing and competing in these games.

Second is success. Teaching juniors is an art, and many standard golf teaching methods and techniques that work quite well for adults may not work at all for juniors. We all know well the importance of technique and standard golf teaching principles. However, it can be easy to forget that kids just want to have fun. When they can have fun playing a game that helps develop specific golf skills, real learning can take place.

2

www.parkitgolf.com

In some ways, we are less concerned with specific technique and more concerned with the outcome. We want each junior to find a way to succeed at these games. Of course, we teach and guide them along the way, but the ultimate objective is to enjoy the process and make playing golf a fun thing to do. There will be plenty of time as kids grow and develop to refine their methods and technique. And, experience has shown that kids playing these games learn more by watching and imitating better players than by rote instruction alone.

The games in this book will make you a successful teacher of junior golfers because they are fun to play and, without realizing it, kids playing the games learn good golf technique, methods, rules, and etiquette.

We encourage you to use *The ParKit Golf Book of Fun Golf Games for Kids* and adapt the games to your specific teaching situation, and have fun doing it!

The ParKit Golf Team is: Diana Law and PGA members Don Law, Rick Heard, Bill Scott, and Chad Kurmel. With more than 90 years of collective experience teaching junior golfers, our team members have won many PGA awards and professional designations, including 2012 National PGA Junior Golf Leader (Don Law), Section Junior Golf Leader (3 times), Chapter Junior Golf Leader (6 times), Section PGA Golf Professional of the Year, Chapter PGA Golf Professional of the Year (3 times), Chapter and Section Bill Strausbaugh Mentor Award, Chapter Horton Smith Education Award (2 times), Chapter Distinguished Service award, US Kids Top 50 Instructor (6 times), US Kids Master Instructor, and Golf Range Top 50 Instructor (4 times).

Editorial note: although we are huge supporters of junior girl golfers, we have used "he" and "his" throughout this book for simplicity.

3

www.parkitgolf.com

PUTTING

COW PASTURE POOL

Overview: This game may be played by 2 or more players. Putting's version of billiards, Cow Pasture Pool helps the student develop:

- ✓ Overall putting skills
- ✓ Strategy and risk-reward thinking in planning the next shot

Equipment Required:

- ✓ 4 ParKit Golf cones or colored string
- ✓ ParKit colored golf balls (4 of each color; 1 color per team)
- ✓ 1 black ParKit Golf "8-ball"

Setup: Please refer to the drawing on the facing page.

➢ Make a boundary using 4 ParKit cones, colored string, or use the entire putting green.

➢ Distribute all of the balls randomly within the boundaries. Place the "8-ball" at the farthest point from the hole.

How To Play:

- Create 2-4 teams (need not be equal size), or play individually. Each player or team is assigned a ball color and must stand outside the boundary behind their assigned cone until it is their turn.

- Select a player or team to go first. Play then continues in a clockwise direction.

- Each player putts one of their assigned colored balls. If the putt is holed, the player continues putting. If not, the player returns to their assigned cone, outside the boundaries. When all of a team's colored balls are holed, they may putt the 8-ball.

- A player may also choose to knock another team's ball either toward or away from the hole. If that ball is holed, the player

www.parkitgolf.com

PUTTING

COW PASTURE POOL

may continue putting. If the other team's ball is knocked outside the boundaries, the ball is considered to be holed for the other team and the player loses his turn.

- While a player is putting, any other player not standing at their assigned cone and outside the boundaries loses his next turn.

- The winner is the first team to hole all of their balls and the 8-ball.

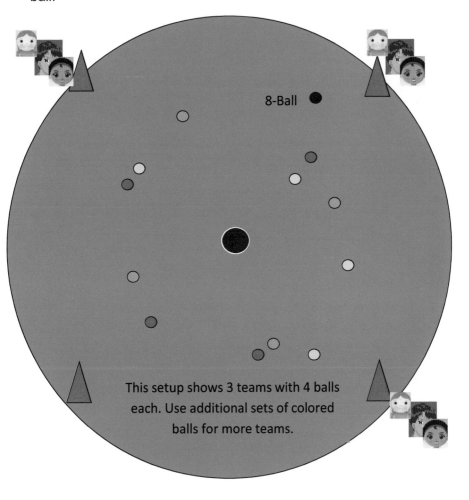

8-Ball

This setup shows 3 teams with 4 balls each. Use additional sets of colored balls for more teams.

www.parkitgolf.com

PUTTING

LAST ONE STANDING

Overview: This game of elimination tests the students':

- ✓ Distance control
- ✓ Ability to focus amid time limits and distractions
- ✓ Ability to remember and follow directions

Equipment Required:

- ✓ 2-5 ParKit Golf cones
- ✓ Colored string (25 feet)
- ✓ ParKit Golf scoring pad
- ✓ Each player needs his own ball, marked for identification

Setup: Please refer to the drawing on the facing page.

- ➢ Stretch string across one side of the putting green. Place 2 ParKit cones approximately 25 feet away from the string.

- ➢ If space permits and teams are used, another set of cones may be placed equidistant from the string on the opposite side from the other cones (as shown in the drawing).

How To Play:

- Create two teams (need not be equal size), or play individually. All players line up between the cones, aiming toward the line. If teams are used, they may line up on opposite sides of the string.

- The instructor will announce "1-2-3… PUTT!", and all players will putt toward the string at the same time. Anyone putting early or late (in instructor's judgment) is eliminated from the round.

- The farthest ball from the string is out, and that player is eliminated (more than one may be eliminated to speed play).

- If teams are used, the teams switch sides for the next round.

www.parkitgolf.com

PUTTING

LAST ONE STANDING

- Players must not leave their putting spot until it has been determined who will be eliminated. Any player who leaves early to retrieve his ball is eliminated in addition to the one farthest from the line.

- The winner is the last player standing.

- Variation: In team play, rather than eliminating a player, the player with the ball *closest* to the string wins a point for the team. Use the ParKit Scoring Pad to keep score. The winner is the first team to reach 10 points.

- Variation: The player closest to the line may choose a player from the other team to be eliminated. When all players for a team are eliminated, the other team wins.

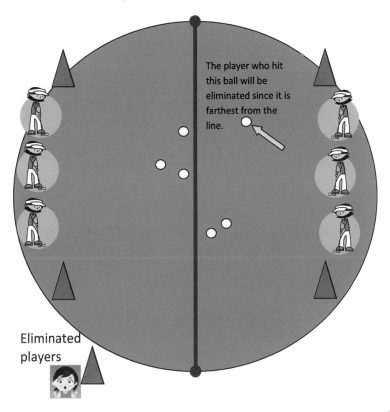

The player who hit this ball will be eliminated since it is farthest from the line.

Eliminated players

www.parkitgolf.com

PUTTING

KNOCKOUT

Overview: This team game helps to develop:

- ✓ Overall putting skills
- ✓ Performance under pressure
- ✓ Decision-making strategy

Equipment Required:

- ✓ 4 ParKit Golf cones
- ✓ 2 ParKit Golf aiming sticks
- ✓ 2 ParKit Golf ball markers

Setup: Please refer to the drawing on the facing page.

- ➢ Place the ParKit ball markers approximately 1 foot apart and 6-8 feet from a hole on the putting green.

- ➢ Place 1 ParKit aiming stick on each side of the ball markers, about 6 feet away where players will await their turn.

- ➢ Away from the hole, place the 4 ParKit cones in a rectangle to be used as a "penalty box".

How To Play:

- Create 2 teams (need not be equal size) and direct each team's players to stand in order behind one of the ParKit aiming sticks. Determine which team will go first. The teams will alternate taking turns. Each team should determine its own order of play.

- Each player will place his ball between the ball markers and putt. If the putt is holed, the player may either:

  1. Choose a player from the other team to go to the penalty box, or

  2. Choose a player from his own team to come back from the penalty box. That player will then putt first on the team's next turn.

8

www.parkitgolf.com

PUTTING

KNOCKOUT

- A player may not be sent to the penalty box for a second time until all of his teammates have also been sent there at least once.

- Once a player has been sent to the penalty box twice, he may not be brought back into the game.

- A team wins when all players from the other team are in the penalty box.

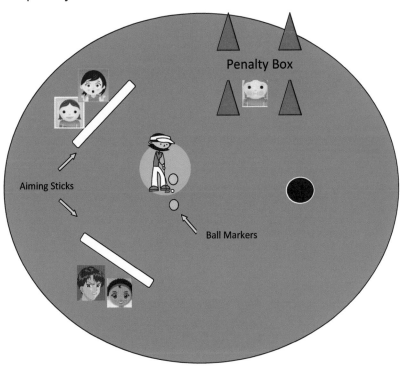

Penalty Box

Aiming Sticks

Ball Markers

www.parkitgolf.com

PUTTING

SCHOOL

Overview: This game for 1 or more players helps to develop:

- ✓ Putting distance control

Equipment Required:

- ✓ 5 ParKit Golf ball markers
- ✓ 1 ParKit Golf 3-foot hoop
- ✓ 1 ParKit Golf cone

Setup: Please refer to the drawing on the facing page.

- ➢ Create a "passing zone" by placing the ParKit 3-foot hoop around the hole as shown. The passing zone begins at the hole and includes the area within the hoop.

- ➢ Beginning 12 inches from the hole, place the ParKit ball markers at 3-foot increments moving away from the hole.

- ➢ Place the ParKit cone where players will await their turn.

- ➢ The closest marker represents "1st grade", the next marker "2nd grade", then "3rd grade", and so on.

How To Play:

- • Determine the order of play among the players. This order will be kept throughout the game. Players wait behind the "on-deck" cone until it is their turn.

- • Each player begins from "1st grade" and putts toward the hole.

- • In order to pass to the next grade, the ball must either go in the hole or finish inside the "passing zone" hoop. If this happens, the player advances to the next grade and putts again. This continues until the player either fails to pass or reaches the highest grade.

10

www.parkitgolf.com

PUTTING

SCHOOL

- If the player fails to pass, he places his ball near that grade ball marker to mark his position. He will return to this grade and again attempt to pass on his next turn.

- The winner is the first player to reach the highest grade, once all players have had an equal number of turns (i.e., when a player reaches the end, any remaining players after him in the round get a chance to tie).

- Ties may be broken by taking turns putting from the highest grade until only one player succeeds in passing.

- The game may be made more challenging by using the smaller 18-inch diameter ParKit hoop or by spacing the markers farther from the hole.

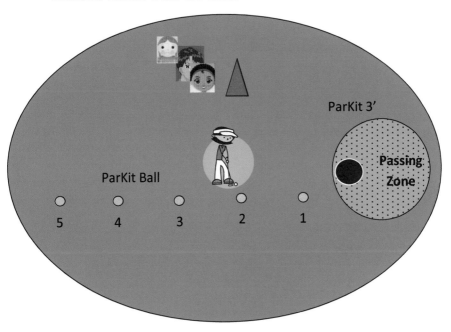

11

www.parkitgolf.com

PUTTING

"21"

Overview: This game for 1 or more players helps develop:

- ✓ Directional control
- ✓ Strategy
- ✓ Mathematical thinking

Equipment Required:

- ✓ 4 ParKit Golf "21" Wickets
- ✓ 2 ParKit Golf ball markers
- ✓ ParKit Golf scoring pad
- ✓ 1 ParKit Golf cone

Setup: Please refer to the drawing on the facing page.

- ➢ Insert each ParKit "21" wicket into the putting green (push wicket in approximately 2 inches). Arrange the "21" wickets in a line, leaving about 6 inches between wickets. You may place the wickets in any order by size.

- ➢ Place the ParKit ball markers about 1 foot apart and approximately 6-8 feet from the "21" wickets.

- ➢ Place the ParKit cone where players will await their turn.

How To Play:

- Determine the order of play among the players. This order will be kept throughout the game. Players wait behind the "on-deck" cone until it is their turn.

- Each player putts from between the ball markers toward the "21"wickets. The "21" wickets are valued at 1 point, 3 points, 5 points, and 7 points. The player decides which wicket to aim for and attempts to putt through the wicket.

12

www.parkitgolf.com

PUTTING

"21"

- If the ball goes through a wicket, the player will receive the point value for that wicket. If any part of the ball goes through a wicket, the player will receive that point value.

- The winner is the first player to reach exactly 21 points.

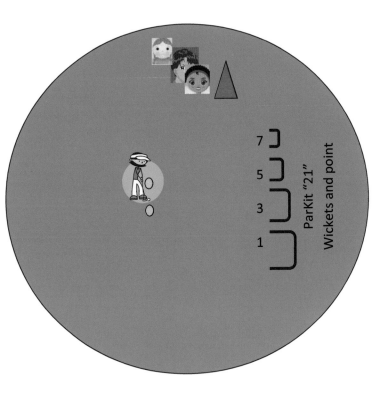

13

CHIPPING

BULLSEYE

Overview: This game for 1 or more players helps develop:

- ✓ Chipping technique
- ✓ Direction and distance control

Equipment Required:

- ✓ 2-4 ParKit Golf hoops
- ✓ ParKit Golf scoring pad
- ✓ 3 ParKit Golf cones

Setup: Please refer to the drawing on the facing page.

- ➢ Place the different sized ParKit hoops around a hole on the putting or chipping green, starting with the smallest hoop.

- ➢ Assign point values to the circles: in the hole is 25 points, smallest circle is 15 points, next circle is 10 points, next circle is 5 points, and largest circle is 1 point (the point assignments and number of circles used may be changed as needed).

- ➢ Place 2 ParKit cones about 6 feet apart, off the green in the area to be used for chipping.

- ➢ Place the other ParKit cone where players will await their turn.

How To Play:

- Determine the order of play among the players. This order will be kept throughout the game. Players wait behind the "on-deck" cone until it is their turn.

- Each player chips 5 balls from between the starting cones toward the hole surrounded by hoops. Keep a running total of the points scored by the player.

14

www.parkitgolf.com

CHIPPING

BULLSEYE

- After the player chips 5 balls, the next player takes his turn.

- The winner is the first player to reach 100 points (or another point total determined by the instructor), once all players have had an equal number of turns (i.e., when a player reaches 100 points, any remaining players after him in the round get a final chance).

- Variation: Use five different chipping stations around the green and assign each player to a station. Each player chips 5 balls, tallies their points, then rotates to the next station. This continues until each player has chipped from each station. The winner is the player with the highest point total after completing the rotation.

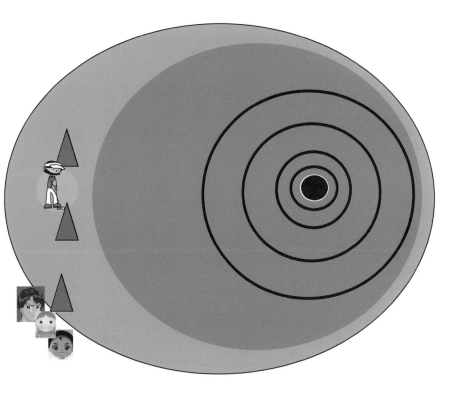

15

www.parkitgolf.com

CHIPPING

CATCH ME (IF YOU CAN)

Overview: This game may be played by 1 or more players or teams, and helps to develop:

- ✓ Chipping distance control

Equipment Required:

- ✓ 6 ParKit Golf cones
- ✓ ParKit Golf scoring pad

Setup: Please refer to the drawing on the facing page.

- ➢ Create a chipping starting point by placing 2 ParKit cones 6 feet apart in a flat area appropriate for chipping up to 30 yards.

- ➢ Create an out-of-bounds limit about 25 yards away from the starting point by placing 3 ParKit cones in line as shown.

- ➢ Place the last ParKit cone where players will await their turn.

How To Play:

- Determine the order of play among the players. Players wait behind the "on-deck" cone until it is their turn.

- The goal is to chip as many balls in a row as possible, where each ball travels farther than the prior ball ("target ball") without going beyond the "out-of-bounds" limit. Each ball must "catch up to" the target ball.

- Each player begins by chipping a ball a short distance, scoring 1 point. That ball becomes the target ball for the next chip. The player then chips a second ball. If that ball catches or passes the target ball, score another point and that ball becomes the new target ball for the next chip.

16

www.parkitgolf.com

CHIPPING

CATCH ME (IF YOU CAN)

- If the chipped ball strikes the target ball, the chip scores a point and the new target ball is whichever ball comes to rest farther from the player.

- Continue chipping until a ball either fails to catch the target ball or the ball goes too far (out-of-bounds). Score a point each time the ball catches or passes the target ball.

- The winner is the player with the most points, once all players have had an equal number of turns.

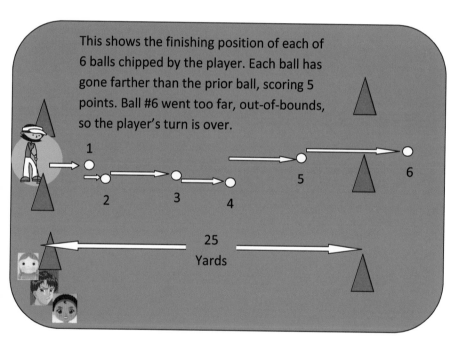

This shows the finishing position of each of 6 balls chipped by the player. Each ball has gone farther than the prior ball, scoring 5 points. Ball #6 went too far, out-of-bounds, so the player's turn is over.

25 Yards

www.parkitgolf.com

CHIPPING

ACE OF CLUBS

Overview: This game may be played by 2 or more players or teams, and helps to develop:

- ✓ Chipping direction and distance control

Equipment Required:

- ✓ 6 ParKit Golf cones
- ✓ ParKit Golf scoring pad
- ✓ 3 ParKit Golf hoops

Setup: Please refer to the drawing on the facing page.

- ➤ Create two chipping stations by placing 2 ParKit cones 6 feet apart for each station, in a flat area appropriate for chipping up to 30 yards. Place a ParKit cone where players will await their turn at each station.

- ➤ Place three different size ParKit hoops: small hoop for a short chip; medium hoop for a medium chip, and large hoop for a long chip.

How To Play:

- • Create two teams (need not be equal sized). Provide an equal number of golf balls (e.g., 10 balls) to each team. Determine which team is to play first.

- • Each team will determine their own order of play. Players wait behind the "on-deck" cone until it is their turn.

- • Alternating shots between teams, each player will chip one ball toward the hoop of their choice, scoring points if the ball comes to rest inside a hoop. Score as follows: 1 point for the small hoop; 2 points for the medium hoop; and 3 points for the large hoop.

18

www.parkitgolf.com

CHIPPING

ACE OF CLUBS

- When all balls have been chipped, the round ends. The winner is the team with the most points. Ties may be broken by continuing to alternate between teams until one team scores more points.

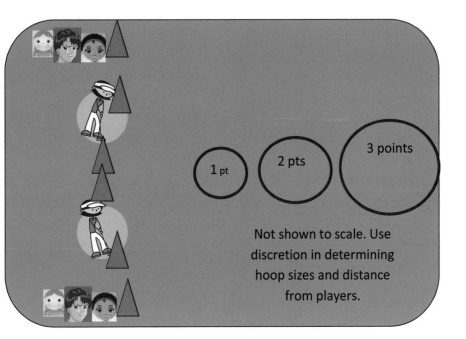

1 pt

2 pts

3 points

Not shown to scale. Use discretion in determining hoop sizes and distance from players.

19

www.parkitgolf.com

CHIPPING

GOLF BOWLS

Overview: This game mimics Lawn Bowls or Bocce, and is excellent for chipping or putting. It may be played by 2 or more players or teams, and helps to develop:

- ✓ Direction and distance control
- ✓ Strategy

Equipment Required:

- ✓ 6 ParKit Golf cones
- ✓ ParKit Golf scoring pad
- ✓ 4 ParKit Golf colored golf balls for each team, plus 1 ParKit Golf black "8-ball".

Setup: Please refer to the drawing on the facing page.

- ➢ Create a chipping station by placing 2 ParKit cones 6 feet apart in a flat area appropriate for chipping up to 30 yards.

- ➢ Place 1-2 ParKit cones where players will await their turn.

- ➢ Place 2 ParKit cones 10 feet apart, 20 yards away from the chipping station to define the far end of the chipping area.

How To Play:

- • Create two teams (need not be equal sized). Each team receives 4 golf balls of the team's color. Determine which team is to play first.

- • Place the ParKit black "8-ball" within the chipping area to be used as the target ball (the "jack" in Bocce).

- • Each team will determine their own order of play. Players wait behind the "on-deck" cone until it is their turn.

20

www.parkitgolf.com

CHIPPING

GOLF BOWLS

- A player from the starting team will chip one ball toward the jack. Then, the other team will chip a ball toward the jack.

- From then on, the team that does not have the ball closest to the jack will chip, until one team has used all 4 balls. At that point, the other team chips its remaining balls, one per player.

- A ball may strike any other ball or the jack, moving either one.

- The team with the closest ball to the jack is the only team that can score points. The scoring team receives one point for each of their balls that is closer to the jack than the closest ball of the other team. The winner is the first team to 7 points.

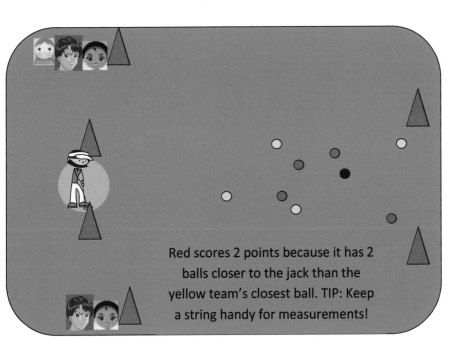

Red scores 2 points because it has 2 balls closer to the jack than the yellow team's closest ball. TIP: Keep a string handy for measurements!

www.parkitgolf.com

CHIPPING

THREE STRIKES

Overview: This game of elimination for 2-6 players helps develop:

- ✓ Direction and distance control
- ✓ Consistency

Equipment Required:

- ✓ Up to 6 ParKit Golf cones (1 per player)
- ✓ 1 ParKit Golf colored golf ball for each player
- ✓ 1 ParKit Golf 18-inch hoop

Setup: Please refer to the drawing on the facing page.

- ➢ Place the ParKit hoop around a hole on the putting or chipping green. The instructor may use judgment and use a larger hoop based on the skill level of the players.

- ➢ Create a chipping station for each player by placing 1 ParKit cone in a flat area appropriate for chipping up to 30 yards. Each player should have a similar lie and angle to the hoop.

- ➢ Each player will use their own white ball, plus a different colored ParKit ball.

How To Play:

- Players go to their chipping stations and prepare to chip their own white ball (ensure balls are marked for identification).

- The instructor will announce "1-2-3... CHIP", and all players will chip at the same time.

- The player whose ball is the farthest white ball from the hole gets a strike (ParKit colored balls do not count for strikes). Any player who chips into the hoop or hole subtracts 1 strike from his total (the minimum strike count is zero).

22

www.parkitgolf.com

CHIPPING

THREE STRIKES

- When a player gets 3 strikes, he is "out" and must change to his ParKit colored ball for subsequent chipping rounds. The player then continues chipping in subsequent rounds, but his colored ball does not count in the measuring for strikes.

- If a player who is "out" chips into the hoop or hole with a colored ball, he changes back to a white ball with 2 strikes and continues competing in subsequent rounds.

- The game is over when there is only one player using a white ball for the start of the next round; that player is the winner.

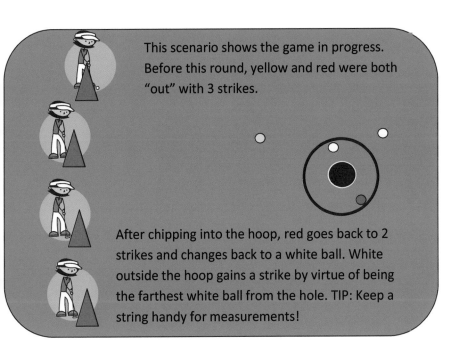

This scenario shows the game in progress. Before this round, yellow and red were both "out" with 3 strikes.

After chipping into the hoop, red goes back to 2 strikes and changes back to a white ball. White outside the hoop gains a strike by virtue of being the farthest white ball from the hole. TIP: Keep a string handy for measurements!

www.parkitgolf.com

PITCHING

AIR MAIL

Overview: This game may be played by 1-5 players or teams, and helps to develop:

- ✓ Pitching technique and distance control

Equipment Required:

- ✓ 6 ParKit Golf cones
- ✓ ParKit Golf scoring pad

Setup: Please refer to the drawing on the facing page.

- ➢ Create a pitching starting point by placing 2 ParKit cones 6 feet apart in a flat area appropriate for pitching up to 40 yards.

- ➢ Create an out-of-bounds limit about 35 yards away from the starting point by placing 3 ParKit cones in line as shown.

- ➢ Place the last ParKit cone where players will await their turn.

How To Play:

- The goal is to pitch as many balls in a row as possible, where each ball travels farther *in the air* than the prior ball ("target ball") without going beyond the "out-of-bounds" limit. Each ball must "air mail" the target ball and stop before going out-of-bounds.

- Determine the order of play among the players. Players wait behind the "on-deck" cone until it is their turn.

- Each player begins by pitching a ball a short distance, scoring 1 point. That ball becomes the target ball for the next pitch. The player then pitches a second ball. If that ball air mails the target ball and stops in bounds, score another point and that ball becomes the new target ball for the next pitch.

www.parkitgolf.com

PITCHING

AIR MAIL

- If the pitched ball strikes the target ball, the pitch scores a point and the new target ball is whichever ball comes to rest farther from the player.

- Continue pitching until a ball either fails to air mail the target ball or the ball goes too far (out-of-bounds). Score a point each time the ball air mails the target ball.

- The winner is the player with the most points, once all players have had an equal number of turns.

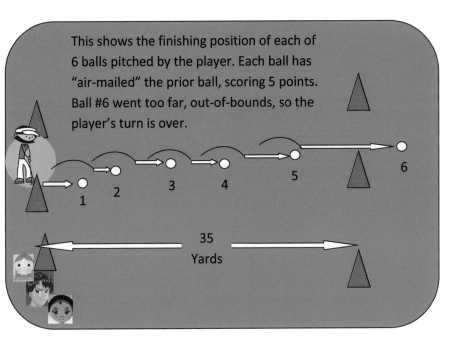

This shows the finishing position of each of 6 balls pitched by the player. Each ball has "air-mailed" the prior ball, scoring 5 points. Ball #6 went too far, out-of-bounds, so the player's turn is over.

35 Yards

www.parkitgolf.com

PITCHING

TIC-TAC-PITCH

Overview: This game may be played individually or in teams (teams need not be of equal size), and helps to develop:

- ✓ Pitching accuracy and distance control
- ✓ Strategy

Equipment Required:

- ✓ 4 ParKit Golf cones
- ✓ 15 ParKit Golf colored golf balls
- ✓ ParKit Golf colored string

Setup: Please refer to the drawing on the facing page.

- ➢ Create a pitching starting point by placing 2 ParKit cones 6 feet apart in a flat area appropriate for pitching up to 20 yards.

- ➢ Place the other ParKit cones where players will await their turn.

- ➢ Create a tic-tac-toe grid by marking 3' X 3' squares with string, turf paint, or chalk.

How To Play:

- Choose sides and play individually with two players, or create two teams (need not be equal sized). Give one side 15 ParKit colored golf balls. The other side will use either white balls or range balls. Determine which side is to play first.

- The game is played like the classic tic-tac-toe Taking turns, each side attempts to pitch a ball into a square on the tic-tac-pitch grid. The first side to pitch into a square claims that square for the side. Claim the square for the side by leaving the player's ball in the square.

www.parkitgolf.com

PITCHING

TIC-TAC-PITCH

- Retrieve and re-use balls as needed to maintain a supply of balls for each team.

- The winner is the first side to make 3 in a row, column, or diagonal (as with tic-tac-toe).

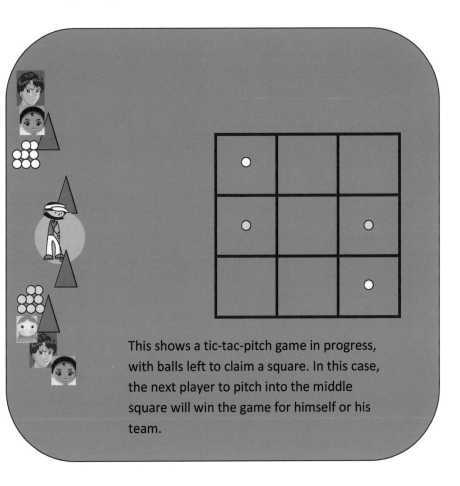

This shows a tic-tac-pitch game in progress, with balls left to claim a square. In this case, the next player to pitch into the middle square will win the game for himself or his team.

www.parkitgolf.com

PITCHING

FLOPPER STOPPER

Overview: This game for 2-6 players helps to develop:

- ✓ Pitching distance control
- ✓ Flop shot technique

Equipment Required:

- ✓ 6 ParKit Golf cones
- ✓ 2 ParKit Golf aiming sticks
- ✓ ParKit Golf scoring pad
- ✓ ParKit Golf colored string

Setup: Please refer to the drawing on the facing page.

- ➢ Create a pitching station by placing 2 ParKit cones 6 feet apart in a flat area appropriate for pitching up to 40 yards.

- ➢ Place 1 ParKit cone where players will await their turn.

- ➢ Place 3 ParKit cones in a line approximately 20 feet away from the pitching station, close enough together so that the ParKit aiming sticks can be placed on top of the cones.

- ➢ Use the ParKit string to create a series of lines parallel to the above 3 cones, spaced every 5 paces from the cones. Assign point values to the spaces within the lines: 1st area is 100 points, 2nd area is 50 points; 3rd area is 10 points.

How To Play:

- • The object of the game is to pitch or flop a ball over the cone and aiming stick barrier and make the ball stop as quickly as possible, scoring the most points.

- • Decide on the order of play. Each player will line up behind the "on-deck" cone until it is their turn to pitch.

www.parkitgolf.com

PITCHING

FLOPPER STOPPER

- Taking turns, each player will pitch 3 balls. The ball must fly over the cone/aiming stick barrier. The player scores points according to where the ball comes to rest, using the point values for each space within the lines.

- The winner is the player with the most points after 3 rounds (the instructor may change the number of rounds).

- The instructor may change the spacing of the lines to make the point scoring areas larger or smaller as needed, depending on the skill level of the players.

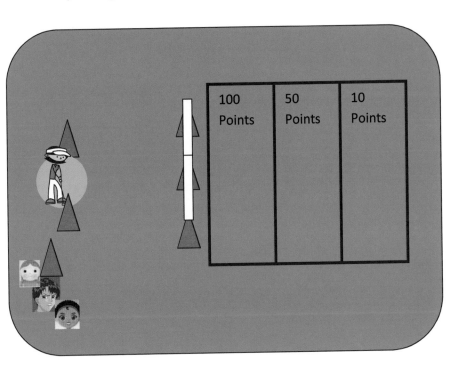

www.parkitgolf.com

PITCHING

POLE VAULT

Overview: This game for 1 or more players helps to develop:

- ✓ Pitching or flop shot technique

Equipment Required:

- ✓ 4 ParKit Golf cones
- ✓ 4 ParKit Golf aiming sticks
- ✓ 1 ParKit Golf banner

Setup: Please refer to the drawing on the facing page.

- ➢ Create a pitching station by placing 2 ParKit cones 6 feet apart in a flat area appropriate for pitching up to 40 yards.

- ➢ Place 1 ParKit cone where players will await their turn.

- ➢ Place the final ParKit cone where players will go when eliminated from the game.

- ➢ Assemble a "pole vault high bar" as follows: First, connect two pairs of aiming sticks, and push each pair of sticks into the ground six feet apart until they are stable. Then, attach the ParKit banner to the top of each pair of aiming sticks. The banner may be slid higher or lower as needed.

How To Play:

- • The object of the game is to pitch or flop a ball over the pole vault high bar (noodle).

- • Decide on the order of play. Each player will line up behind the "on-deck" cone until it is their turn to pitch.

- • Taking turns, each player will attempt to pitch a ball over the high bar. If successful, that player advances to the next round. If not, that player is eliminated.

30

www.parkitgolf.com

PITCHING

POLE VAULT

- After the round is complete, if 2 or more players remain in the game, the tee marker cones are moved closer to the high bar, and the players again attempt to pitch a ball over the bar.

- The winner is the player who successfully pitches a ball over the high bar from the closest point to the bar. If neither player is successful, additional rounds may be played until only one player succeeds in clearing the high bar.

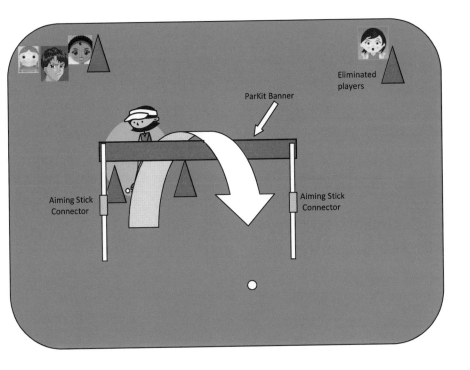

31

www.parkitgolf.com

PITCHING

SHOOTOUT

Overview: This elimination game for 2 or more players helps develop:

- ✓ Pitching technique
- ✓ Direction and distance control
- ✓ Etiquette in order of play
- ✓ Strategy in approaching shots from different angles and situations

Equipment Required:

- ✓ 6 ParKit Golf cones
- ✓ ParKit Golf scoring pad

Setup: Please refer to the drawing on the facing page.

➢ Place the ParKit cones in six different locations around the practice green. Try to select locations that represent typical and challenging pitch or flop shot situations that a player may experience on the course.

How To Play:

- Determine the order of play among the players.

- Beginning at one of the ParKit cones, each player hits one shot toward the hole.

- Assign points to each player based on their ball's distance from the hole. The farthest away gets one point, the next closest gets 2 points, etc. If there are four players, the closest gets 4 points. Keep each player's point tally on the ParKit scoring pad.

- All players then move to the next ParKit cone for the next round, and scoring continues until all players have hit from each cone.

www.parkitgolf.com

PITCHING

SHOOTOUT

- The winner is the player with the most points after all players have played from each cone. Ties may be broken by a final shootout from one of the cones, with the closest player to the hole being the winner.

- If desired, the instructor may choose to use fewer than six pitching locations.

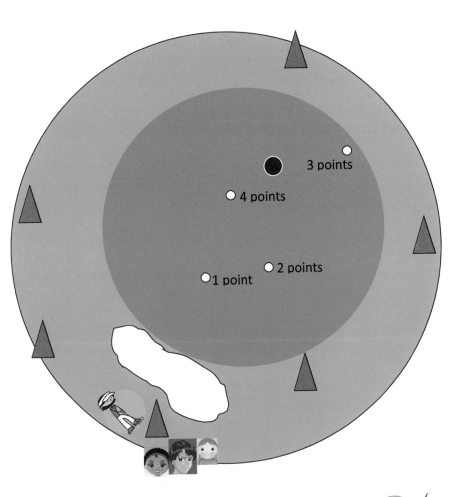

www.parkitgolf.com

BUNKERS

RELAY RACE

Overview: This team game helps develop:

- ✓ Instinctive shotmaking, without becoming preoccupied with technique

Equipment Required:

- ✓ 5 ParKit Golf cones
- ✓ ParKit Golf scoring pad

Setup: Please refer to the drawing on the facing page.

- ➤ Make two bunker stations by placing two ParKit cones in the bunker, spaced far enough apart to allow two players to hit shots simultaneously. Next to each cone, place 8 golf balls.

- ➤ Place the other two ParKit cones out of the bunker where each team will await its turn.

- ➤ Place the final ParKit cone as an aiming aid for the players.

How To Play:

- Create two teams (need not be equal sized). Determine which team is to play first. Each team will determine its own order of play. Players wait behind the "on-deck" cone until it is their turn.

- Make sure it is clear which team is to use which bunker station.

- When the instructor says "GO", player #1 from each team runs into the bunker to hit a ball. Each player gets two attempts to hit one ball out of the bunker toward the aiming cone. If the player fails to hit the ball out, the player must throw it out of the bunker.

- Once the ball is out of the bunker, the player will run back to his team and tag the next player. This player will hit the next ball and the rotation will continue until one team has no balls remaining.

34

www.parkitgolf.com

BUNKERS

RELAY RACE

- When one team's balls are all out of the bunker, that team wins the round and scores one point.

- The teams then return to their respective on-deck cones and the instructor resets the bunker stations with eight golf balls for the next round.

- The winner is the first team to reach 5 points.

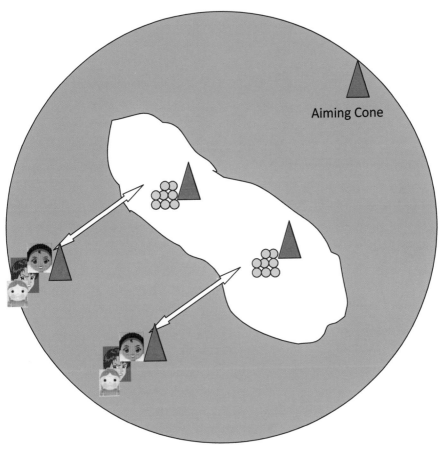

35

www.parkitgolf.com

BUNKERS

SEQUENCE

Overview: This game for two or more players helps develop:

- ✓ Consistent bunker technique
- ✓ Performance under pressure

Equipment Required:

- ✓ 4 ParKit Golf cones
- ✓ 1 ParKit Golf large hoop (optional)
- ✓ ParKit Golf scoring pad

Setup: Please refer to the drawing on the facing page.

➢ Make a bunker station by placing two ParKit cones about 6 feet apart in the bunker. Place a supply of golf balls in the station.

➢ Place one ParKit cone where players will await their turn.

➢ Place the final ParKit cone as a target for the players. Optionally, use the ParKit hoop for advanced players.

How To Play:

- Determine the order of play. Players wait behind the "on-deck" cone until it is their turn.

- Define the goal for the players. For beginners, the goal is simply getting a ball out of the bunker. For more advanced players, the goal may be defined as stopping a ball within the ParKit hoop or meeting some other criterion.

- Following the order of play, each player will take a turn hitting bunker shots toward the target. If the player scores a goal (as defined above), he continues until he fails to score.

- Each ball that scores a goal counts as one point. The player's turn ends when he fails to score.

36

www.parkitgolf.com

BUNKERS

SEQUENCE

- The winner is the player who scores the most points.

- The game may be played with more than one round, in order to have a winner for each round, plus an overall winner.

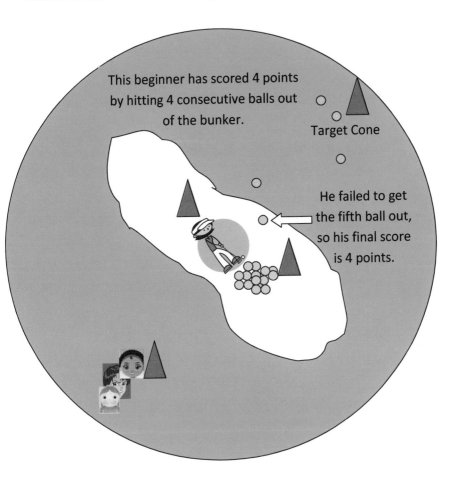

This beginner has scored 4 points by hitting 4 consecutive balls out of the bunker.

Target Cone

He failed to get the fifth ball out, so his final score is 4 points.

www.parkitgolf.com

BUNKERS

ESCAPE ARTIST

Overview: This game for 2 or more players helps develop:

- ✓ Advanced bunker skills for handling difficult lies.

Equipment Required:

- ✓ 1-5 ParKit Golf cones
- ✓ 1 ParKit Golf large hoop

Setup: Please refer to the drawing on the facing page.

- ➤ Place six golf balls in difficult lies in the bunker (e.g., "fried egg", buried, rake furrow, footprint, side hill, downhill, etc.).

- ➤ Place one ParKit cone where players will await their turn.

- ➤ If the practice bunker is not near a green, place four ParKit cones in a rectangle, representing a green-sized target area for intermediate skill level players.

- ➤ Place the ParKit hoop as a target for advanced skill level players.

How To Play:

- • Determine the order of play among the players.

- • Following the order of play, players will take turns attempting to hit a ball out of the bunker from a difficult lie.

- • The winner is the first player to get three balls out of the bunker.

- • For intermediate skill level players, the winner is the first player to get three balls to stay on the green or, if no green is available, within the cone rectangle.

38

www.parkitgolf.com

BUNKERS

ESCAPE ARTIST

- For advanced players, the winner is the first player to get three balls to stop within the hoop.

- The instructor may optionally require the players to use two or more different clubs to hit the bunker shots.

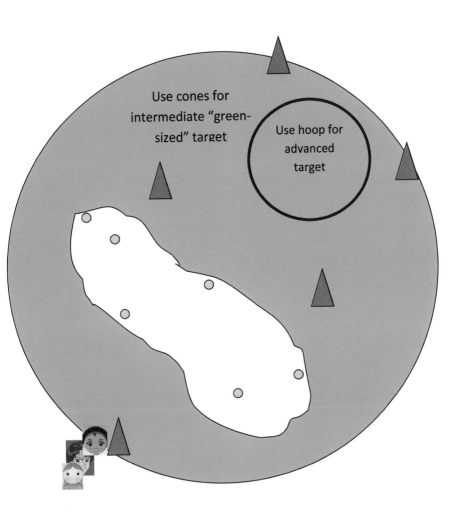

Use cones for intermediate "green-sized" target

Use hoop for advanced target

39

www.parkitgolf.com

BUNKERS

KING OF THE BUNKER

Overview: This game for 2 or more players helps develop:

- ✓ Bunker shot direction and distance control.

Equipment Required:

- ✓ 3 ParKit Golf cones
- ✓ 3 ParKit Golf hoops (small, medium, large)

Setup: Please refer to the drawing on the facing page.

- ➤ Make a bunker station by placing two ParKit cones about 6 feet apart in the bunker. Place a supply of golf balls in the station.

- ➤ Place one ParKit cone where players will await their turn.

- ➤ Place three ParKit hoops at increasing distances from the bunker, beginning with the smallest hoop, then the medium hoop, then the large hoop (use your judgment on distances from the bunker).

How To Play:

- Determine the order of play among the players.

- Following the order of play, players will take turns attempting to hit a ball out of the bunker into each of the hoops.

- In order to win the game, a player must hit, in any order, one ball anywhere out of the bunker, and one ball into each of the hoops.

- The winner is the first player to complete all four requirements.

- For lesser skilled players, the game may be modified by using only the largest hoops. Alternatively, only one or two hoops may be used to simplify the game.

www.parkitgolf.com

BUNKERS

KING OF THE BUNKER

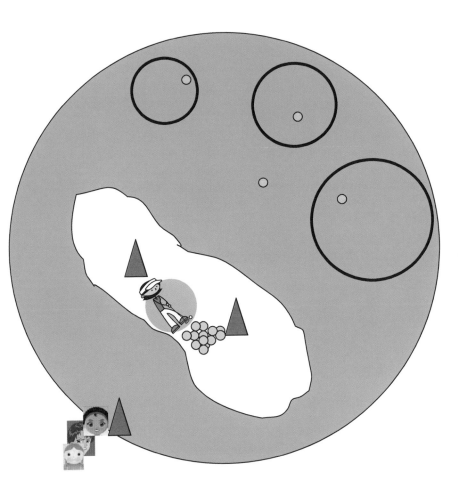

www.parkitgolf.com

BUNKERS

BUNKER LADDER

Overview: This game for 2 or more players helps develop:

- ✓ Bunker shot direction and distance control.

Equipment Required:

- ✓ 3 ParKit Golf cones
- ✓ 6 ParKit Golf aiming sticks
- ✓ ParKit Golf scoring pad

Setup: Please refer to the drawing on the facing page.

- ➢ Make a bunker station by placing two ParKit cones about 6 feet apart in the bunker. Place a supply of golf balls in the station.

- ➢ Place one ParKit cone where players will await their turn.

- ➢ Beginning about 5 yards from the bunker, insert one ParKit aiming stick into the ground. Moving in a zig-zag pattern, insert the remaining aiming sticks in 5 yard increments moving away from the bunker (see drawing).

How To Play:

- Determine the order of play among the players.

- Following the order of play, players will take turns attempting to hit a ball out of the bunker toward one of the aiming sticks that the instructor has designated for each round.

- Players receive points based on their rank order proximity to the designated aiming stick. For example, if there are 5 players, the player closest to the aiming stick receives 5 points; the next closest receives 4 points, etc., and the farthest away receives 1 point.

- Any player who fails to get the ball out of the bunker receives 1 point, regardless of proximity to the aiming stick.

42

www.parkitgolf.com

BUNKERS

BUNKER LADDER

- Players must keep track of their own point total after each round.

- The winner is the player with the most points after six rounds (one round for each aiming stick "ladder rung").

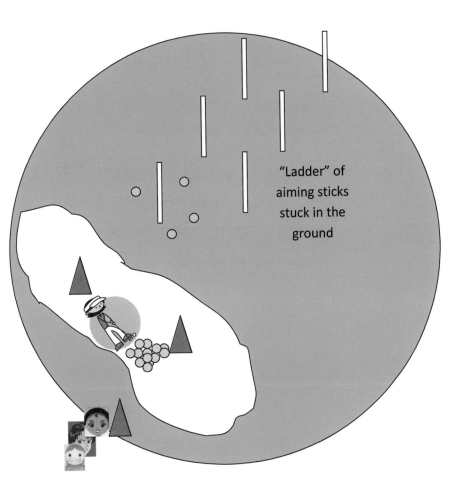

"Ladder" of aiming sticks stuck in the ground

43

www.parkitgolf.com

FULL SWING

HOME RUN DERBY

<u>Overview</u>: This team game helps develop:

- ✓ Consistency in hitting full shots
- ✓ Performance under pressure

Equipment Required:

- ✓ 6 ParKit Golf cones
- ✓ 4 ParKit Golf aiming sticks
- ✓ ParKit Golf scoring pad

<u>Setup</u>: Please refer to the drawing on the facing page.

> ➢ Make a full swing station by aligning two ParKit aiming sticks about 6 feet apart on the practice tee suitable for full driver shots. Place a supply of golf balls in the station.

> ➢ Place one ParKit cone for each team, where players will await their turn.

> ➢ Create a "home run fence" by using two ParKit aiming sticks for the left and right field foul poles and arranging four ParKit cones to represent the outfield fence. The instructor should use judgment in deciding how far away the "fence" should be.

How To Play:

- Create two teams (need not be equal sized). Determine which team is to play first. Each team will determine its "batting order". Players wait behind their "on-deck" cone until it is their turn.

- Decide in advance how many "innings" will be played.

- Taking turns, the teams "come to bat" following their team "batting order". Each player attempts to hit a ball over the "fence" in the air. If successful, one "run" is scored.

44

www.parkitgolf.com

FULL SWING

HOME RUN DERBY

- If the ball does not clear the "fence" or is a "foul ball" (outside the aiming stick "foul poles", the team gets an "out". After 3 "outs", the "inning" is over and the other team "comes to bat".

- The winner is the team with the most runs after the agreed-upon number of innings.

"Home Run" Fence

Aiming stick
"foul pole"

Aiming stick
"foul pole"

www.parkitgolf.com

FULL SWING

TOWER OF POWER

Overview: This game for 2 or more players helps develop:

- ✓ Full swing aim
- ✓ Ball trajectory control
- ✓ Instinctive shotmaking, without becoming preoccupied with technique

Equipment Required:

- ✓ 5 ParKit Golf cones
- ✓ ParKit Golf scoring pad
- ✓ 6 or more plastic range ball baskets (not in ParKit kit)

Setup: Please refer to the drawing on the facing page.

> ➤ Make two full swing stations by placing three ParKit cones in line about 6 feet apart on the practice tee suitable for full driver shots. Place a supply of golf balls in each station.

> ➤ Place one ParKit cone for each team, where players will await their turn.

> ➤ Construct the "tower of power" by stacking the plastic range ball baskets on top of one another in a pyramid as shown. WARNING: DO NOT USE METAL RANGE BASKETS FOR THIS GAME!

How To Play:

- Create two teams (need not be equal sized). Each team will determine its order of play. Players wait behind their "on-deck" cone until it is their turn.

- One student from each team will enter their hitting station. When the instructor says "GO", both players will hit 5 balls at the "tower of power". The goal is to knock the tower down. The first player to knock down part or all of the tower earns a point for their team.

46

www.parkitgolf.com

FULL SWING

TOWER OF POWER

- After the first round of players have hit 5 balls, they return to the "on deck" area and the next player from each team takes a turn.

- If a player hits more than one ball at a time, he loses the round and the other team gets one point.

- The winner is the team with the most points after all players have had a turn.

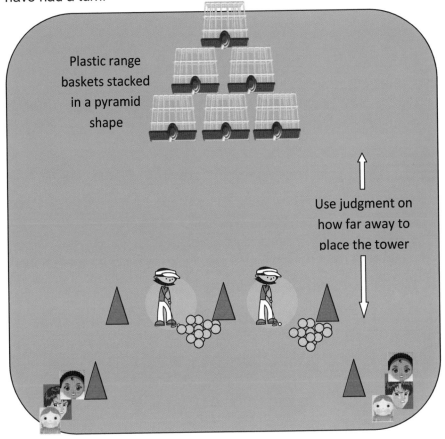

Plastic range baskets stacked in a pyramid shape

Use judgment on how far away to place the tower

www.parkitgolf.com

FULL SWING

_G-O-L-F_

Overview: This game for 2 or more players helps develop:

- ✓ Full swing advanced shot shaping and ball control

Equipment Required:

- ✓ 3 ParKit Golf cones
- ✓ ParKit Golf scoring pad

Setup: Please refer to the drawing on the facing page.

- ➢ Make a full swing station by placing two ParKit cones about 6 feet apart on the practice tee suitable for full driver shots. Place a supply of golf balls in the station.

- ➢ Place one ParKit cone where players will await their turn.

How To Play:

- Determine the order of play among the players.

- Following the order of play, players will take turns following the directions of the instructor.

- The instructor will state what club the first player must use.

- The instructor will also describe the type of shot to hit (e.g., a hook, slice, straight, high, low, or medium trajectory shot).

- If the player does not successfully execute the required shot, he gets the next letter of the word "G-O-L-F", and the instructor selects the shot for the next player in line.

- If the player does successfully execute the required shot (to the satisfaction of the instructor), the player selects the type of shot for the next player in line.

- If that player does not successfully execute the shot, he gets a letter. If he does, he then selects the shot for the next player, and so on.

www.parkitgolf.com

FULL SWING

G-O-L-F

- When a player accumulates all of the letters G-O-L-F, he is out of the game.

- The winner is the last player remaining.

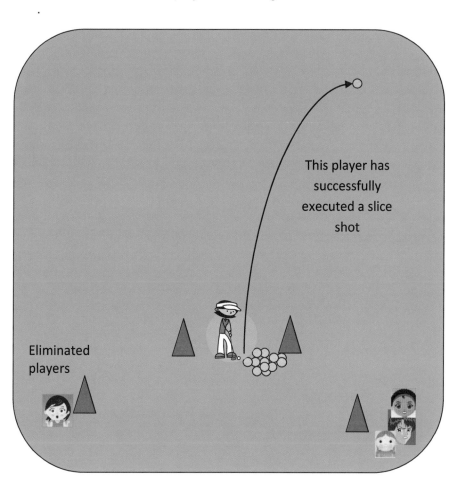

This player has successfully executed a slice shot

Eliminated players

www.parkitgolf.com

FULL SWING

PRESSURE COOKER

Overview: This game for two or more players helps develop:

- ✓ Consistent full swing shotmaking technique
- ✓ Performance under pressure

Equipment Required:

- ✓ 5 ParKit Golf cones
- ✓ 2 ParKit Golf aiming sticks
- ✓ ParKit Golf scoring pad

Setup: Please refer to the drawing on the facing page.

- ➢ Make a full swing station by aligning two ParKit aiming sticks about 6 feet apart on the practice tee suitable for full shots. Place a supply of golf balls in the station.

- ➢ Place one ParKit cone where players will await their turn.

- ➢ Place four ParKit cones in a rectangular shape on the range or hitting area a suitable distance from the hitting station, depending upon the club to be used for full shots and the skill level of the players. These cones will be used to define the target area for full shots, so place them defining a large target area such as a green or fairway (see drawing).

How To Play:

- Determine the order of play. Players wait behind the "on-deck" cone until it is their turn.

- Define the goal for the players as a shot that lands within the target area marked by the four cones.

- Following the order of play, each player will take a turn hitting shots toward the target area. If the player's ball lands within the target area, he scores one point and continues until he hits a ball that does not land within the target area.

www.parkitgolf.com

FULL SWING

PRESSURE COOKER

- Each ball that scores a goal counts as one point. The player's turn ends when he fails to score.

- The winner is the player who scores the most points after everyone has had an equal number of turns.

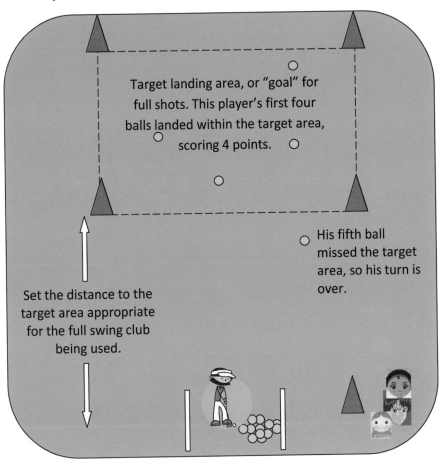

Target landing area, or "goal" for full shots. This player's first four balls landed within the target area, scoring 4 points.

His fifth ball missed the target area, so his turn is over.

Set the distance to the target area appropriate for the full swing club being used.

51

www.parkitgolf.com

FULL SWING

VIRTUAL GOLF

Overview: This game for two or more players helps develop:

- ✓ Full swing shotmaking technique
- ✓ Club selection and shot strategy
- ✓ Etiquette in order of play
- ✓ Rules in dealing with hazards, out-of-bounds, etc.

Equipment Required:

- ✓ 1-2 ParKit Golf cones
- ✓ 2 ParKit Golf aiming sticks
- ✓ ParKit Golf scoring pad

Setup: Please refer to the drawing on the facing page.

- ➤ Make a full swing station by aligning two ParKit aiming sticks about 6 feet apart on the practice tee suitable for full shots. Place a supply of golf balls in the station.

- ➤ Place one ParKit cone where players will await their turn.

- ➤ Use your imagination to describe a golf hole as viewed from the full swing station. Describe the fairway, any imaginary bunkers, trees, dogleg shape, hazards, and green location. Players will "play" this "hole", so ensure each player understands your vision of the hole.

How To Play:

- Determine the order of play. Players wait behind the "on-deck" cone until it is their turn.

- Following the order of play, each player will select a club and "tee off" on the imaginary hole, remembering where their ball comes to rest.

- After each player has teed off, players will prepare to hit their second shot. Based on the location of their tee shot and following the rules of golf, each player will select a new club

52

FULL SWING

VIRTUAL GOLF

appropriate for their next shot and play the "hole" as described by the instructor, always hitting from the full swing station. Play continues until all players are "on the green".

- The winner is the player to reach the imaginary "green" in the least number of shots.

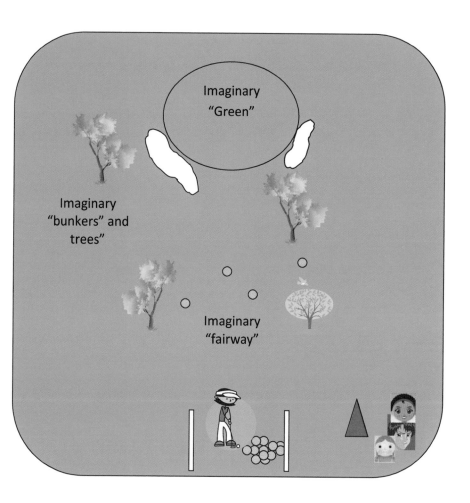

www.parkitgolf.com

Made in the USA
Lexington, KY
02 August 2014